VICTORY

—— THROUGH THE ——

VALLEY

KEITH MARKS

authorHOUSE®

AuthorHouse™
1663 Liberty Drive
Bloomington, IN 47403
www.authorhouse.com
Phone: 1 (800) 839-8640

Published by AuthorHouse 04/17/2017

ISBN: 978-1-5246-0815-6 (sc)
ISBN: 978-1-5246-0814-9 (e)

Print information available on the last page.

Any people depicted in stock imagery provided by Thinkstock are models, and such images are being used for illustrative purposes only. Certain stock imagery © Thinkstock.

This book is printed on acid-free paper.

Because of the dynamic nature of the Internet, any web addresses or links contained in this book may have changed since publication and may no longer be valid. The views expressed in this work are solely those of the author and do not necessarily reflect the views of the publisher, and the publisher hereby disclaims any responsibility for them.

Scripture quotations marked KJV are from the Holy Bible, King James Version (Authorized Version). First published in 1611. Quoted from the KJV Classic Reference Bible, Copyright © 1983 by The Zondervan Corporation.

From A Victim to Victory

Apostle Keith Marks is an advocate of suffering, taught by life experiences, overcomer of many obstacles, opposition, and demonic opponents, by the principles and precepts of God. Apostle Keith Marks has witnessed the hand of God bring him through life turbulences and tribulations by building a tabernacle for God to come and release his power. Apostle Keith has traveled from valley to victory by the grace of God. The process of victory will be painful. There will be problems, pressures, and persecutions but this is what God utilizes to bring promotion.

CONTENTS

CHAPTER 1

I'm In the Fight of My Life

BATTLES ARE INEVITABLE in this walk with God; there is no victory without a battle. Life will usher you through so many battles. At some point, you won't be able to comprehend how you will make it through. What determines the victory is not the strength that you obtain but who is going to fight the battle. At times, you can be in the fight of your life and utilize every strategy, method, or plan to fight, only to lose and become frustrated and disappointed. Resulting in the option to give up.

It's an uncompromising conclusion that, at some point in this christian journey, we all must embrace spiritual combat. Satan will utilize his best strategies to block our progress and to stop us from successfully reaching victory. As Daniel 7:25a notes "And he shall speak great words against the most High, and shall wear out the saints of the most high". Thus, the enemy will launch antagonistic attacks to divert you and to thwart your persistence in reaching the promise. He will multiply frustrations purposefully to steal your focus so that the future will be forfeited.

As Christians, we are created to be spiritual containers that house victory. However, many times we find ourselves in positions where we win some battles and lose others. There will be an opponent who will come to obliterate our opportunities, oppose our open doors, and penetrate the open portals to prevent promotion. Victory will not be obtained alone; their must be a team effort for victory.

God led the children of Israel by the prophetic voice of the prophet Moses from the wilderness of sin into Rephidim. God led the people from the wild places into a place of rest. Even in the place of rest, difficulty of division, discord, and discouragement were present. The people of God rose up against Moses; in actuality, they came up against the authority of God. It is a dangerous thing to come up against the authority that God has given to his servants. When the people came to test God through his servant's authority, he released the spirit of the Amalekites, which was the spirit of war.

It was the responsibility of Moses to prepare the victory for the children of Israel. In Exodus 17:8–13 "Then came Amalek, and fought with Israel in Rephidim. 9. And Moses said unto Joshua, Choose us out men, and go out, fight with Amalek: tomorrow I will stand on the top of the hill with the rod of God in mine hand. 10. So Joshua did as Moses had said to him, and fought with Amalek: and Moses, Aaron, and Hur went up to the top of the hill. 11. And it came to pass, when Moses held up his hand, that Israel prevailed: and when he let down his hand, Amalek prevailed. 12. But Moses' hands were heavy; and they took a stone, and put it under him, and he sat thereon; and Aaron and Hur stayed up his hands, the one on the one side, and the other on the other side; and his hands were steady until the going down of the sun. 13. And Joshua discomfited Amalek and his people with the edge of the sword." It doesn't matter what kind of attacks you face, what matters most is that you have an anointing to partake of the victory. It's through Jesus Christ that we gain strength for the victory, as Paul writes in 1 Corinthians 15:57–58 "But thanks be to God, which giveth us the victory through our Lord Jesus Christ. 58. Therefore, my beloved brethren, be ye steadfast, unmovable, always abounding in the work of the Lord, forasmuch as ye know that your labor is not in vain in the Lord." Obtaining true victory lies in one's ability to sustain strength in the midst of the struggle. Strength is not an outward appearance but an inward endurance. Strength is exercised under the weight of pressures. Survival mode is not acceptable when you are destined for success; obliviously, God trains us with trials, and it's the training through the trials that results in triumph in troubles.

God has always intended for his people to walk in authority and victory over the enemy. Activating and accessing God's spiritual weaponry is essential for victory. Psalm 27:2 proclaims, "When the wicked, even mine enemies and my foes, came upon me to eat up my flesh, they stumbled and fell." God has equipped us with spiritual instruments, instructions, and insight to destroy the methods of the enemy; According to Psalm 144:1 "Blessed be the LORD my strength, which teaches my hands to war, and my fingers to fight." It's impossible to partake of the promise if the principles are avoided. As a prerequisite of victory, the responsibility of participation in fighting the war is rooted in activating the spiritual arsenal with the anointing. The fight must be waged according to God's will, way, work, and word. The apostle reminds us in 1 Timothy 1:18 "This charge I commit unto thee, son Timothy, according to the prophecies which went before on thee, that thou by them mightest war a good warfare." Timothy was charged; the word *charge* means to instruct authoritatively, to refuse to give up under pressure, pain, problems, or persecutions. In this light, learning to endure means to undergo hardship without giving up. We are to endure as soldiers. We read, "Thou, therefore, endure hardness, as a good soldier of Jesus Christ" (2 Timothy 2:3).

What happens when the enemy that you're fighting comes from the inside? God wants to teach us strategies for the victory that will be won in the battle. When the attacks of the Amalekites came pursuing Moses, he had to strategize. He had to evaluate, eliminate, or elevate everybody before engaging in the execution of the enemy. Everything was created to have a relationship. Relationships play a vital role in possessing victory. Moses had to make a choice of who would go to battle with him. In Exodus 17:8–10; Then came Amalek, and fought with Israel in Rephidim. 9. And Moses said unto Joshua, Choose us out men, and go out, fight with Amalek: tomorrow I will stand on the top of the hill with the rod of God in mine hand. 10. So Joshua did as Moses had said to him, and fought with Amalek: and Moses, Aaron, and Hur went up to the top of the hill; We were created to have not merely a relationship but the right relationship and placement in our lives.

To ensure the maximum and fullest potential, the right placement as it relates to the relationship is significant. You can be connected to the right people, but if they are not in the proper positions in your life, your circumstances can be as bad as being connected to the wrong people. It is important to evaluate everybody who has a connection with you and to ask about the motives of the relationships. Question the integrity of the relationship: "Is it going to help me or hinder me?" Sometimes taking an honest assessment can help discover everybody said it's not reliable. The people rose up against Moses the prophet, testing his authority and tempting God. This released the warring spirit against Israel. Rebellion against God's plans opens up satanic doors and motivates unnecessary warfare that can be avoided. Moses realized that he had to place the right people around him. He had to evaluate those who were around him to recognize what they were capable of doing.

Some people are dead weight; they can harm you more than they help in the time of battle. During the battle, Moses didn't have time to play games; his life was on the line. Moses came to the conclusion that he had to evaluate and then eliminate, meaning he had to move some people away from the place where they would not produce victory. Moses didn't just do these things on his own; he requested insight from Joshua. He asked Joshua to choose men to go and to fight. The name Joshua is another form of Jesus, meaning "he saves." Joshua didn't just place people in the proper positions in his life. Moses allowed Joshua (Jesus) or the spirit to choose who would be eliminated and who would be elevated.

When letting people into your space, you have to be led by the Spirit. The same people who will say that they are for you will turn their backs on you. Require relationships with people who are there for the long haul, people who will not give up under pressure. The people you eliminate from your life will get upset. Not everyone is destined to go with you into battle; some are just not equipped for the fight. Moses allowed the spirit to choose whom he had to eliminate. You will have people who will get angry when God tells you to eliminate them. If there is a need for an explanation, you have to tell them that

God eliminated them. The Spirit did as Moses asked, and they were evaluated; some were eliminated from Moses's presence when Joshua went down and fought in the trenches.

Sometimes God has to create a circumstance to show who is genuinely equipped and who should be eliminated. All types of people will surround you; it's only revealed in the heat of the battle in which positions they must be placed. When your life is on the line, make sure that you have the right relationships with the people who are close to you. Most often it's the ones who are close who will kill you. As Moses listened to the Spirit, God showed him whom he needed to eliminate from his presence, and the ones besides Joshua whom he eliminated were sent to the valley.

Make sure that you never make the mistake of trying to elevate a valley or a low-level relationship. In Exodus 17:9 we read that Joshua was sent to oversee every person who was not worthy to be elevated. They were sent out of Moses's presence. Moses discovered a principle to which that we all need to gravitate and to adopt: get all the low-level relationships out of your life. Moses learned a lesson we can learn too: people will disrespect the anointing on your life. The people had shown their hand by rebelling against Moses, so he said that not everyone could be in his. Moses suffered dearly for his anointing; he discovers something about people, if they disrespect you once they will do it again. You can't afford to have thirty- fold people in your space. Don't allow thirty- fold people around you in the heat of your battle, eliminate those that are haters, jealous, selfish, gossipers, and noisy they become distractors. Out of everybody that was around Moses only two were elevated with him. God will allow or orchestrate situations that cause a separation when it's time for elevation. Remember where God is taking you, everybody can't go.

CHAPTER 2

DEMONIC ATTACKS AGAINST THE ANOINTING OF YOUR AUTHORITY

THERE IS A situation that caused a separation right before Moses' elevation, meaning an indication that God is getting ready to elevate when He starts to separate the low-level people out of your life. Antagonistic attacks will come against the anointing of your authority. In Exodus 17:10-12a "So Joshua did as Moses had said to him, and fought with Amalek: and Moses, Aaron, and Hur went up to the top of the hill. 11. And it came to pass, when Moses held up his hand, that Israel prevailed: and when he let down his hand, Amalek prevailed. 12. But Moses' hands were heavy, and they took a stone and put it under him, and he sat thereon; and Aaron and Hur stayed up his hands, the one on the one side, and the other on the other side; and his hands were steady until the going down of the sun; While Joshua and the rest of the warriors were in the valley in a battle Moses, Aaron, and Hur went up on the hill with the rod of God in Moses' hand.

Moses recognizes that he has eliminated all of the thirty-fold people out of his life and takes Aaron and Hur up with him on the mountain, when spiritual warfare comes, methodically go up in the realms of the spirit and fight. Moses has two that were one hundred-fold people who went up to the mountain with him. It is not only how it is done in the natural war; some are battling physically in the valley but hidden within the frameworks of this text is revealed a spiritual war also. Immature christians can fight in the valley and not recognize the physicality of the war Ephesians 6:12 "For we wrestle not against flesh and blood, but against principalities, against powers, against the rulers of the darkness of this world, against spiritual wickedness in high places."

There is a deeper revelation in the text that must be revealed to understand what this battle is really about. Moses says were going up on the hill with the rod of God in my hand in verse 9. All of this to the spiritual eye unveils that the battle isn't just physical it now has become a spiritual war. The going up in the hills represents the realms of the spirit in the heavens; the rod represents Gods authority, and His hand represents victory, fellowship, might, and power. Spiritually the hand represents the five-fold ministry: the Apostles, Prophets, Pastors, Evangelist, and Teachers. The Bible never says his arm gets tired, but it says his hands go up and down. The 21st-century church needs to know that we're not fighting each other, but the spirit of the amalekites has been released within the body of Christ. Which is resulting in the complaining. Complaining about the things of God is the doorway that releases the warring amalekites spirit that causes an attack on the authority of the five-fold ministry in the church.

There is an attack on the authority of the five-fold ministry. Whenever the leader has delegated authority to those that can handle it, there will always be a warring spirit that will rebel against that authority. Some ask questions, why did they tell her to tell me, or you, not the Pastor, who do they think that they are? On the job when the supervisor gives a command, everybody falls in line However when it's done in the church there is always a fight. It is the wiles of the enemy that we must recognize those that are attacking the rod or the authority of God. Recognize the strategies of the enemy, it's not an attack on you, but it is an attack to strip away the authority that God has given to you. That's why you must go up into the realms of the spirit as Moses did in Acts 1:8 "But ye shall receive power, after that the Holy Ghost comes upon you: and ye shall be witnesses unto me both in Jerusalem, and in all Judaea, and in Samaria, and unto the uttermost part of the earth." This power is to release the anointing for ministry, authority to operate and function in the government of God, might for spiritual warfare and dominion to reign over the devil.

The Amalekites spirit doesn't come to attack you, but it comes to attack your God given authority. The enemy may come up against the God in you but Matthew 16:18

declares "And I also say unto thee, that thou art Peter, and upon this rock I will build my church; and the gates of hell shall not prevail against it." Even hell itself will not overthrow the kingdom of God. Be careful and cautious when coming up against the plan of God; You may not understand, who are even why God chooses a particular person but you're not coming up against the person you coming up against God, your arms are too short to fight against the power of God. God releases his anointing on whom he chooses, and you have to be careful how you handle or mishandle His anointed one. In Acts 5:39 "But if it is of God, ye cannot overthrow it; lest haply ye be found even to fight against God." You don't know who God has anointed for his kingdom advancement he says in Psalm 105:15 "Saying, Touch not mine anointed, and do my prophets no harm. You can't put your mouth on God anointed one, gossip about them, or set up traps, he says touch not. When you touch his anointing, it will cause you your death, read about Uzzah in 2 Samuel 6:7 that when he touched the anointing, he was struck with death.

The weariness will come to wear out your worship while in spiritual warfare in verse 11 it states "and it came to pass, when Moses held up his hand, that Israel prevailed; and when he let down his hand, the Amalek prevailed in verse 12. But Moses hands were heavy, and they took a stone and put it under him, and he sat thereon; and Aaron and

Hur stayed up his hands, the one on the one side, and the other on the other side; And his hands were steady until the going down of the sun 13. And Joshua discomfited Amalek and his people with the edge of the sword. The bible says that Moses has the rod of God in his hand and his hands get heavy." Moses is in the presence of God, it's only when you have allowed the Spirit of God to kill your flesh that you can get in God's presence.

When you get in the holy of holies, around the ark of the covenant, which represents the presence of God there are three things the golden pot of manna, Aaron rod that budded and the 10 commandments inside the ark of the covenant. He has supernatural provision because they are highly outnumbered, he has the rod of God which represents the authority of God, the authority to send Joshua to fight, the word Joshua means Jesus, everything must bow to the name Jesus and the Ten Commandments meaning the word. Now the word means revelation, the fact that he has both hands up means he has a double portion of revelation. Moses is in the presence of God in the hundred fold realm; both hands are up meaning he has a double anointing. He has Aaron his priest with him and Hur in the masculine derivative noun the name Hur means to burn or ignite. So that Moses has the priest in Aaron, the Holy Ghost in Hur and the presence of God, he is in fellowship with the Father, Son, and Holy Spirit. The bible says because Aaron and Hur were with him on a high spiritual level that they get the revelation that as long as our leader's hands are up they win but when his hands fall down they would lose. There is a need for more spiritually minded people to have an eye to see in the spirit as it relates to leaders. Moses never opened his mouth to tell them that his hands were heavy, they were mature enough to discern that their leader was tired. They also discerned that they had to do something to keep his hands up. If leaders are not strengthen, they lose the battle. Moses was tired of fighting and exhausted his strength in the spirit; he has people in position around him that see his weakness, and they cover him by keeping his hands lifted.

They are in the realm with Moses they see and discern that he is weak, didn't ask but they see what needed to be done, and they do it without being asked. Moses didn't inform them that he was weak, he didn't request for them to hold his up hands up. They see their leader's weakness, and they cover him by keeping him on the stone it represents the presence of God. They cover his weakness by holding his hands up as a result of them keeping his hands up they win the battle. They see that Moses is tired in his spirit, and so they lifted him up. I wonder if you see a co-labour tired in the spirit or your leader will you lift him up. They didn't give lip service, the problem is that there are too many people in the church that just talk, talk is cheap.

We should walk out what we talk about. Aaron and Hur didn't open their mouth they just ran and assisted their leader by keeping him in God's presence. How does one keep their leader in the presence of God? By assisting and doing whatever your hands find to do, in prayer and don't just talk about it, be about it. Secondly, they kept his hands up. Hand represents authority, and the lifting of hands represent spiritually keep. The level of authority, in fact, that has been set in the house, is for keeping the order.

Moses has his people with him; he has two young men that are going to keep both of his hands up, meaning keep the standard of authority and order lifted that has been set in the house. Moses had in his hand Aaron rod that budded and blossomed; budding represents the fruit is here so that Moses has the fruit if his labor, he has two young men that see his weakness, but they don't go in for the kill, they don't strip him, but they strengthen his authority. Can you see someone weakness and not destroy their character our integrity in their moment of weakness. Now these were two young men that were on the same level as Moses, but they didn't disrespect him, they knew their position. Know your place and position. Their man of God was weak they could have killed him and taken over but they didn't. Leaders needs sons and daughters, that are good fruit, not rotten or corrupt fruit, so that when you see the enemy coming in to test the authority that has already been set in the house that you will raise up to the enemy and say we are not going to allow anything contrary to the authority of the leader. The fruit of the leader's labor is to lift up the authority that God has set in the house, when the amalekite spirit comes to war against the authority that has been set.

When you hear the thirty-fold people say to lift my hands up they respond by saying, "We don't do that here", "I don't agree with the Pastor", "I'm not doing it as he says," or say "why don't we do it like this or that". This type of behavior sow seeds of discord and causes chaos. When the leader is absent, the assignment is to maintain the leader's mission. They keep his hands lifted while he was weak until the sun goes down, which meant they keep Moses hands up until a new day and new season of strength came. As long as the young men kept the leaders hand of authority lifted, Joshua won the battle and defeated the Amalekites and their people with the sword. Exodus 17:13 says "And Joshua discomfited Amalek and his people with the edge of the sword. God wants us to know that if we keep the authority and order of the house, as a standard, that this battle isn't even ours. I told you that the word Joshua means Jesus, and Jesus will fight our every battle with the sword of the word. If we keep our hand of authority. The Lord does not desire fear to grip the soul and cripple the assignment, 2 Chronicles 20:15b "Thus saith the LORD unto you, Be not afraid nor dismayed by reason of this great multitude; for the battle is not yours, but God's."

Understand that God will repay every adversary and enemy for satanic ploys, plans and plots launched to bring destruction Isaiah 59:19b "When the enemy shall come in like a flood, the Spirit of the LORD shall lift up a standard against him." We must refuse to be afraid of the enemy! Psalm 37:1-2 "Fret not thyself because of evildoers, neither be thou envious against the workers of iniquity. 2. For they shall soon be cut down like the grass, and wither as the green herb." God will deal with our enemy we must keep our eyes stayed on him Isaiah 26:3 "Thou wilt keep him in perfect peace, whose mind is stayed on thee: because he trusteth in thee."

CHAPTER 3

I'M WALKING OUT OF THIS WITH THE VICTORY

THOSE OF US that are a part of the death, burial and resurrection of our Lord and Savior Jesus Christ learns early in life, when presented the right opportunity it can stop you right in your tracks. Life is full of unexpected twist and tremendous turns, it will lead you down paths against your will to the point that if life doesn't change, ultimately life will change us. It can matriculate through adversity, associations, and afflictions, all of these can prevent you from being zealous in the things of God and stagnant your desire to serve God.

Walking through life is a progressive forward movement in the natural that assist us from one place to another. However, many have found it true to be stuck, stagnated and at a complete standstill through becoming comfortable in a complex situation. Many have learned to adapt to dysfunction as functional. Change can be challenging, but it is vitally necessary, we must resist the opportunity to forfeit our future to familiarity, and pursue the plan of God. We must come to the realization in the spirit, that's if we are going to be successful in life, we must adhere to the spirit and not our situation. Most often than not the promises of God can be misleading at times. We have misdiagnosed the totality of the requirements that our Lord and Savior ask of the believer. When God releases a promise that the plans to the promise are not always predicated or beneficial to our feelings and emotions. Everything that we have, all that we are, all that we shall become, all hang upon the hinges of our faith being rooted in the foundation of the promises of our God.

The greater the promise, the greater the fight, emphatically, some of the promises are irrevocable, you will not enjoy the summation of the promise without suffering the agony of antagonistic attacks, the distractions of diabolical delusions with almost snapping, crackling and popping, before you walk into what God has prepared and promised you. There will be times in life to where after dealing with cycles of horrific events that you will ask the question how long will it be before I get out of this, I'm not seeing what God has said. The psychological mind sends a warning that says I don't know how much more of this I can put up with. You began to breakdown and not breakthrough. So then now the struggle within the confinements of our finite mind intensifies, and you come to the conclusion that what you're dealing with isn't normal and that the difficulties that are in the pathway of life that your soul has to admit that these attacks have to be of the devil.

You walk around with a smile on your face and a frown in your heart; you have tried to settle and fit in with those around you and adapt to the environment. We are surrounded by people that are dealing with pressures and diabolical attacks that appear to be inhumane in their walk to the promise, that's trying to hold you hostage to your situation. It's in most situations and struggles that God requires us to be obedient through the act of faith. We have to hear God and follow each instruction precisely to get the results that God desires for us. It is in the awkwardness of his essence that it seems as if he matriculates our mind. It is the irony of God. All of life difficulties aren't always of the devil; God will use satan in the process, sometimes difficulties are birth out of an individual flaws, and selfish choices. One has to deal with accepting Gods decisions that he makes for our life without Him asking for our permission. While juggling the fruit of the choices that has been made. It's only when a settlement and comfortability where God maneuvers us, the individual, in the valley of decision that forces a choice to be made. We must submit to God.

God will yoke you to a place of making choices that will stretch you into responsibilities and accountabilities that you were not ready to deal with. It seems as if God waits until you are settled in the possibilities of compromising that he strikes us with another challenge John 5:1-9 "After this there was a feast of the Jews, and Jesus went up to Jerusalem. 2. Now there is at Jerusalem by the sheep market a pool, which is called in the Hebrew tongue Bethesda, having five porches. 3. In these lay a great multitude of impotent folk, of blind, halt, withered, waiting for the moving of the water. 4. For an angel went down at a certain season into the pool, and troubled the water: whosoever then first after the troubling of the water stepped in was made whole of whatsoever disease he had. 5. And a certain man was there, which had an infirmity thirty and eight years. 6. When Jesus saw him lie, and knew that he had been now a long time, in that case, he saith unto him, Wilt thou be made whole? 7. The impotent man answered him, Sir, I have no man, when the water is troubled, to put me into the pool: but while I am coming, another steppeth down before me. 8. Jesus saith unto him, Rise, take up thy bed and walk. 9. And immediately the man was made whole, and took up his bed, and walked: and on the same day was the sabbath". We see this man that has been on his bed of affliction for 38 years; he has all kind of situations against him, but he makes up his mind that today I'm walking out of this. You have to have a made up mind. Know that there is triumph in the turbulence of trouble. The bible says that Jesus came to Jerusalem for a Jewish feast to the sheep gate called

Bethesda, which is the house of mercy and grace; it had 5 porches, that were used as coverings for the multitudes that were sick as they waited for the move of the water. This pool was a place where the sheep and men would go in and kneel down to drink of the water. The only way one could drink of the pool was that they knelt down, which is a sign of humility. The bible explains that this was a place for accommodating sick people, blind, lame, withered and impotent people not only were they sick.

Once the man got to the pool because of the design of the pool, without healing he would become trapped. The pool was 30 feet below sea level and 40 feet back under the mountain. They were not only withered dried up and shrunken their lifestyle didn't measure up to Gods standard. To be blind metaphorically speaks of having no vision, they couldn't see in the spirit. Being paralyze was equivalent to not moving and progressing in the things of God, impotent relating to being non-productive. They were trapped, but with all of their issues God still covers them. Humility with your issue will allow God to give the grace and mercy to cover you even when you don't measure up. Have you ever fell into something that was easy to fall into and hard to get out of ? You know the stuff your body led you into that your mouth couldn't get you out of. Have you ever been trapped in something and couldn't get out? Trapped in the spirit and wanted to walk out of? The cravings of flesh have had you trapped.

The bible explains it had five porches; five is the number of grace, goodness and mercy. Thank God for his mercy, that he didn't bring death when sickness came, God keeps his people covered. Even though they were in the midst of being sick, weak, withered, and halt they were waiting for the moving of the water. Water represents the spirit, and if the spirit doesn't move, one will remain trapped. You might say I'm trapped, weak, unproductive, but wait on the spirit, when the spirit arrives, he brings liberty. When the spirit arrives, it gives sight to the blind, power to the impotent, momentum to the halt and expansion to the withered. It's vital to get into his presence when the presence of The Lord shows up things have to turn around. John 5:4 "For an angel went down at a certain season into the pool, and troubled the water: whosoever then first after the troubling of the water stepped in was made whole of whatsoever disease he had." The devil that caused the trouble, it is utilized as the handy work of God. It's in the troubling of trials that God will allow us to triumph in tragedy it brings us to the greatest deliverance. The troubles and agitations carry deliverance. Deliverance means to snatch out of what has imprisoned you. God has given instructions to avoid certain things, people and places. When instructions are not followed God has to send a shaking in the spirit. If God wouldn't have agitated, stirred or troubled the water of the wrong relationship, you never would have gotten out the draining friendship, and it revealed to you who was really for you. He orchestrated a situation to reveal people's real motive.

We must thank God for the troubles and turbulences that causes of to detach from somethings, and walk into the deliverence. Jesus never shows up while it's calm, he shows up when the water is troubled. If there is no troubling, there is no need for his presence, no trouble no victory and triumph. Psalm 46:1 "God is our refuge and strength, a very present help in trouble". We have misinterpreted the scripture it didn't say whosoever stepped in first which indicates only one would get healed, meaning God would be bias if it says whosoever first stepped in which indicates you can put your hand in first, arm in first if you put anything else in beside your feet first you were disqualified. If you rolled in, but all and who ever walked in on their feet, whoever got in the pool on their feet first were made whole, the man was on his back and needed someone to get him on his feet. You couldn't step in before the troubling, can't do it while the pool was calm. It's in the trouble that God wants you to stand. If you walk in it every part of your body walking is walking in deliverance. That's why the enemy doesn't want you to walk in it, Joshua 1:3 "Every place that the sole of your foot shall tread upon, that have I given unto you, as I said unto Moses." It's the armor of God that will give strength in the midst of the struggle Ephesians 6:13 "Wherefore take unto you the whole armor of God, that ye may be able to withstand in the evil day, and to have done all, to stand."

CHAPTER 4

A WEAPON FOR YOUR WEAKNESS

AFTER DEALING WITH issues a long time you can become immune to them. The bible states that this certain man has had an infirmity for 38 years and when Jesus looks at him it was something about him that let Jesus know that this man has been wrestling with this issue for quite some time. What it is that's creeping out of the crevices of your demeanor that's releasing the clues that you been wrestling with your issue for a long time and you have given into your weakness? Some of us have been wrestling with our weakness, so long that we have given into it and have allowed the dysfunction of it to become a normality!

When Jesus sees him lying, an indication that he has been there for a while is because he is on his mat. His mat has become a part of his life for 38 years. Whenever you see the man you always see the mat and whenever you see the mat you always see the man. His issue has become a part of him. I wonder what issues do you have that you wrestled with so long that you have given in to your issue, and it has now become a part of you. This man had his infirmity for a long time. John 5:5-7 "and a certain man was there, who had an infirmity thirty-eight years. 6. When Jesus saw him lying, and knowing that he had spent much time, He said to him, do you desire to be made whole? 7. The infirm man answered Him, Sir, when the water is troubled, I have no one to put me into the pool." But while I am coming, another steps down before me. It may be a struggle however it's still your responsibility to fight, wrestle, and fight for deliverance.

The thing about being in a fight for your life is that you don't care whose watching. You don't have time to be embarrassed when you are fighting for your life. When you are struggling to win this battle you can't be concerned about what's going on around you. We come to church week after week embarrassed about people seeing us get delivered. This man wasn't embarrassed, but why? It was a public infirmary, meaning that it's a place for impotent, unproductive, blind, and withered people verse 5 says, this man had an infirmity and weakness.

The house of God is a public infirmary, public means everybody can see, the fact that you show up to the house of God doesn't exempt you from weakness. I've never seen in the body of Christ to where the people come and always point out the weakness of others. The fact is that we all are in need for the spiritual hospital, all of us has a weakness. Some try to hide the weakness of anger, the flesh, fornication, sin, or pride but Jesus ask the question in verse 6 that makes the man take responsibility for choosing whether or not he has a sincere desire to let it go. He asks him do you have a desire to do better. You have some people that will complain about a weakness but don't have a desire for change. They have fallen in love with their bed of affliction; they don't want nor are they willing to give up the weakness. Some people are always talking about they want out, in reality, they love their weakness.

They have gotten comfortable with it. Jesus ask the man look stop playing games do you want to get up? As long as you will tolerate it, you will never change it. When you get sick and tired is when you will take the initiative to get up, it's by any means necessary! Stop letting the weakness wear you out. The man had gotten comfortable, look at his reply to Jesus in verse 7 he says when the water is trouble I haven't got anybody to put me in. An indication that you have fallen in love with your weakness and dysfunction is when help is offered you make up excuses. People that make an excuse is a waste of time don't allow anybody to waste precious time making excuses. Time is valuable. Either you want to let go, or you don't. Now it's a difference when you want to let go, and it won't let go of you, than to just simply love the thing that's making you weaker and weaker and still won't let go is insane. Weaknesses become weights, and weights will hold you down. The man wants to hold on, so he makes excuses. You have to let go. Jesus asked all the prerequisite he just asked do you want to rid yourself of this weakness? Are you willing to let it go? Let go of the weights that weighing on you, past pain, how they lied to you, ran your name in the mud, hurt your feelings and tried to destroy your character. Lay aside the weights that tries to hinder you in Hebrews 12:1-2 "Wherefore seeing we also are compassed about with so great a cloud of witnesses, let us lay aside every weight, and the sin which doth so easily beset us, and let us run with patience the race that is set before us, 2. Looking unto Jesus the author and finisher of our faith; who for the joy that was set before him endured the cross, despising the shame, and is set down at the right hand of the throne of God."

All contrary circumstances will cease and crumble under the hand of Christ John 5:6-9 "When Jesus saw him lie, and knew that he had been now a long time in that case, he saith unto him, Wilt thou be made whole? 7. The impotent man answered him, Sir, I have no man, when the water is troubled, to put me into the pool: but while I am coming, another steppeth down before me. 8. Jesus saith unto him, Rise, take up thy bed, and walk. 9. And immediately the man was made whole, and took up his bed, and walked: and on the same day was the sabbath."

No matter what the circumstances whispers everything has to come subject to the subduing power of Jesus. Jesus asks the man a question to see if he wants deliverance, Wilt thou be made whole? The question was an evaluation for elevation. Jesus is fully aware of the man circumstances, and how long he has been in predicament. He ask the man, regardless of how he looks, he asked him, did he want to be made hold? It has to be the will of man for Jesus to move. Jesus didn't comfort his circumstance he confronted the credibility of his character. Jesus says don't play me like you playing everybody else; Jesus confronts his character before he corrects the circumstances, so do you want to get up? Jesus says do you know who I am, I already know about all your circumstances, I know you're in a bad environment not conducive for you, you have been here 38 years, nobody will put you in the pool, people always step in before you, you around people with no vision, not progressing, weaker than you, and people that are stuck.

Jesus knew all of what the man was going through, He came to confront and change his character, and the way I'm confronting your character is I have a question, do you want to get up, if you do get up and walk. God is confronting some of us, he says don't give me the stipulations of your circumstances, just get up, and walk. Jesus says I can't comfort what's wrong; I will confront what's wrong to make you a conqueror. Jesus tells him you are blaming everybody else, but the real issue doesn't have anything to do with everybody else, the issue is that you have gotten comfortable, and the question is do you have enough faith to believe.

When destiny is calling, it's no time to be stuck in a weakness. Jesus tells him to get up and gives him the power to get up. Through the words that came out of his mouth, but the man had to be willing to get up in Isaiah 55:11 "So shall my word be that goeth forth out of my mouth: it shall not return unto me void, but it shall accomplish that which I please, and it shall prosper in the thing whereto I sent it. He has to make an effort." You will find strength in your struggle; God will give you the strength to carry what's been weighing on you. In verse seven the man was complaining and verse eight Jesus says I'm taking control and crushing all of your circumstances. You have the character of a conqueror. Jesus says show me the champion in you; he says get up. Jesus says I have your circumstances under control, because of me the circumstances don't matter. No matter what you are dealing with or going through or what people say when God open up a door the circumstances don't matter.

It doesn't matter where you come from, what you did when God in the picture the wrong circumstances don't matter. Circumstances can't hinder what God has for you. Every conqueror has the complications of circumstances. The challenges in life are to prove that you are a conqueror. Your strength is in your struggle and the fact that you're a conquerer is proven in your complications. When the man hears the word something shifts in the man, The word speaks and says get up, and the words speak to his faith Romans 10:17 "So then faith cometh by hearing, and hearing by the word of God." The more he hears the word, the more strength the man gets, the man starts acting and walking in the character of a conqueror, Paul says in Romans 8:37 "Nay, in all these things we are more than conquerors through him that loved us." Somebody has wondered is there a plan to get me out of the misery of my mess, how will my mistakes fit in with my miracle? God says there is a miracle in your mess, there is power in the word of God.

God is getting ready to correct your circumstances. Jesus says it doesn't matter what the circumstances are because He is bread in a starving land, water in dry places, doctor on the operating table, a judge in the courtroom, an enemy to your enemy and your deliverer. The Bible says that when the man gets his word the man snatched the character of a conqueror and took up his bed and walked, he didn't ask, but he took. Don't ask anymore, put a demand on what the word says, Matthew 11:12 "And from the days of John the Baptist until now the kingdom of heaven suffereth violence, and the violent take it by force."

Get up and take control of your life, control your atmosphere, control your finances, mind, flesh, circumstances, families, demonic forces, and even generational curses. It doesn't matter where you are, rather water in dry places, bread in starving lands In verses 8-10 as long as his bed was carrying him it was fine but when the champion over the circumstance began to carry it, it became unlawful. Long as you was laying in the bed of drugs, it's cool but soon as you lay aside every weight and carry it folk start talking.

Refuse to worry about the circumstances, there will always be situations. However Jesus will handle them that's not for you to worry about, he has given you power in the word; Do you want to get up and stay up? I'm walking out of my circumstances with the victory. I will no longer be a victim of my circumstances.

CHAPTER 5

YOU'RE UP FOR PROMOTION

HIDDEN WITHIN THE heart of the human race is found in appetite that craves more. It's this appetite that becomes the driving force that supplies the demand that creates a longing for fame, riches and power. No one desire to drive the same car for years, live in the same house forever, wear the same wardrobe for more than six months, simply to say many have an appetite for more, experience upgrade and walk into greatness. Titles, positions, stilettos, suits and even clergy collars will not solidify who we were created to be in God. Emphatically within the body of Christ people are in position and there is an absent of power.

There are outward decorations in walking in no real deliverance and power. Having the accolades with no real anointing. There are those that are called that have coped out to be cheap carbon copies, cheap duplicates then those that has been destined for greatness. Some have been disguised as duplicates for the refusal to walk through the process of receiving the hand of God upon their lives in 1 Samuel 17:55-58 "And when Saul saw David go forth against the Philistine, he said unto Abner, the captain of the host, Abner, whose son is this youth? And Abner said,

As thy soul liveth, O king, I cannot tell. 56. And the king said, Enquire thou whose son the stripling is. 57. And as David returned from the slaughter of the Philistine, Abner took him, and brought him before Saul with the head of the Philistine in his hand.58. And Saul said to him, Whose son art thou, thou young man? And David answered, I am the son of thy servant Jesse the Bethlehemite."

The church is being stripped of the authenticity of what God has predestined to produce lasting results of healing and deliverance. Many are mesmerized by only talents and gift, which has robbed God of his glory. The authentic anointing of God must be tried in the fire, tested by temptations, and proven through persecutions. When a person is exempt from going through the proper channels of the process that fulfill Gods purpose, they become procrastinators, and the heavens label them as counterfeits. It does not matter what your name is among men; the true identity is the weight that you carry in the heavens.

When the atmosphere has been stirred up to release what God has already spoken, hell can't stop it. It is the anointing that God releases upon your mantle that declares that you're greatly significant in the Kingdom. A sign that the kingdom has been released is through signs, wonders and miracles in Matthew 16:17-18 "And Jesus answered and said unto him, Blessed art thou, Simon Barjona: for flesh and blood hath not revealed it unto thee, but my Father which is in heaven. 18. And I say also unto thee, That thou art Peter, and upon this rock I will build my church; and the gates of hell shall not prevail against it."

If God doesn't promote you there will be a lack of signs, miracles and wonders. David is now ready for promotion, and there are a few principals that David wants to teach us we that must do if we are going to get recognize by God for promotion. Pursuing God's instructions places you in a position to be promoted 1 Samuel 17:17-20 "And Jesse said unto David his son, Take now for thy brethren an ephah of this parched corn, and these ten loaves, and run to the camp to thy brethren; 18. And carry these ten cheeses unto the captain of their thousand, and look how thy brethren fare, and take their pledge.19. Now Saul, and they, and all the men of Israel, were in the valley of Elah, fighting with the Philistines. 20. And David rose up early in the morning, and left the sheep with a keeper, and took, and went, as Jesse had commanded him; and he came to the trench, as the host was going forth to the fight, and shouted for the battle." He arrived at the camp just as the Israelites were going out to their battle line, shouting the war cry.

When it comes time for promotion everyone wants the position; The prerequisite is to picked, prepared and have the patience to be elevated. God calls many, but only a few are chosen, selected and picked by God in Matthew 22:14 "For many are called, but few are chosen." The chosen of

God are not determined by perfections but is determined by the pureness of the heart. David has many imperfections, but the pureness of his heart overrode his imperfections. David is elevated as a result of his servant's heart. God will never elevate you to your full potential in the Kingdom of God if you don't have a heart that is pure and a heart to serve his greatest asset which is His people Acts 13:22 "And when he had removed him, he raised up unto them David to be their king; to whom also, he gave testimony, and said, I have found David the son of Jesse, a man after my own heart, which shall fulfil all my will." When God finds a man after his heart that can adhere to His instructions he knows that he will execute them precisely. David has been instructed by his father to go and take his brother food in verse 20 David did exactly what he was commissioned to do without questioning his instructor.

The problem in the body of Christ is that majority of servants don't want to follow the instructions that are given to them without rebelling secretly by questioning those that are in authority. David never questions one thing that his father instructs him to do; he does exactly what his assignment required. The promotion will not come if instructions are not followed, the directions given by those that are in authority over you. It doesn't matter how anointed, gifted or talented an individual is instructions must be followed. People in the body of Christ rebel and reject instructions openly and expect promotion. Many claim to be in the kingdom of God and rebel against the will of God.

When a position opens, they get upset and murmur when God chooses not to elevate them. If you want to be promoted in the kingdom of God, you have to be submitted to the instructions of spiritual authority, because it in the submitting that God examines your heart. When were not obedient, then we're not ready to be promoted because we can't follow simple instructions. God has given us simple instructions to love each other, be faithful over time, talents, treasures, obey them that rule over us, get out of flesh and walk in the spirit. It's our obedience that open doors. We will not get the promotion until we can follow the blueprint that our spiritual upper management hands down without questioning their authority. Isaiah 1:19 "If ye be willing and obedient, ye shall eat the good of the land." If David would have been disobedient to his father he would never have been placed in the position to see Goliath, and bring him down which gives him elevation. How many opportunities for promotion have been forfeited for disobedience?

Whenever you are obedient God can trust you, and when God can trust you, he will elevate you. God wants to know can He trust you with trials, persecutions, temptations, power, and long suffering. You will never get a promotion if God can't trust you to follow his instructions. Be properly prepared to put to death the persecution of your peers 1 Samuel 17: 28-31 "And Eliab his eldest brother heard when he spake unto the men; and Eliab's anger was kindled against David, and he said, Why camest thou down hither? And with whom hast thou left those few sheep in the wilderness? I know thy pride, and the naughtiness of thine heart; for thou art come down that thou mightiest see the battle. 29. And David said, what have I now done? Is there not a cause? 30. And he turned from him toward another, and spake after the same manner: and the people answered him again after the former manner. 31. And when the words were heard which David spake, they rehearsed them before Saul: and he sent for him. Have you ever discovered that as long as you were out in the wilderness you were not bothered, but it's when God has his hand on you and promotes you persecution knocks at your front door." David is following the instructions of his father, he takes the food to the camp of his brothers, just the presence of David causes havoc.

When there is an anointing on your life, intimidation shows up when your presence enters the room. Don't be misdiagnose by the spirit of intimidation. Don't get in your feelings when people are intimidated by the anointing on your life; it's just an indication that you have already been anointed for promotion and the position. People get so upset as a result of looking face to face with their replacement. People are intimidated because they have the position with no power. They are outdated, and you are their new replacement. It's David's brothers Eliab that deals with the spirit of intimidation. Eliab is a reubenite and has a son name Danthan. Jacob tells all his boys the spirit that they will walk in during their life. He tells Reuben that he will have a spirit of wanting to be important (Genesis 49:4), the tribe of Dan will operate in a spirit of a poisonous snake on the side of the road that will bite the hill of the horse to throw its rider off backward (Genesis 49:17). Eliab has two spirits wanting to be important and like a snake that catching you off guard and biting you to release the poison that will throw you off focus and cause you to backslide. Whenever the spirit of intimidation is evident in a person, they have to release poison on you to bring you down because they can't come up to where you are.

The strategy the enemy uses to bring you down to their level when your up for promotion is persecution. Persecution means to harass with oppressive treatment. David's brothers attacked him with persecution because David shows up for his divine appointment. Eliab gets angry and asks what are you doing here and who is taking care of the sheep in the wilderness. When promotion is in your life, the devil will use anybody to cause persecution in your life. Eliab tells David you don't have a right to be here; this is not your place, you're not good enough to be in this position go back to where you were at the bottom of the wilderness.

The devil is a liar! God in this season is removing all of the diluted, watered down people out of the way and replacing the outdated with those that are anointed with the pure power of God.

Eliab instructs David to go back to the bottom; he brings up his past not realizing it's his past that birthed the anointing. Don't be embarrassed when the enemy tries to reveal your wilderness experience, be reminded it's what you went through in the wilderness that causes you to be anointed. David doesn't let the persecutors hinder his promotion. Eliab was in the position but wasn't doing anything because he was afraid. That same spirit still lingers in the Body of Christ; people are in a position that won't produce and don't want you to do anything either. David didn't stop like Eliab; he confronted the spirit, and the Bible says he turned, and kept asking questions. Be prepared for persecution from peers when God is promoting you, everybody is not going to be excited for you in 1 Samuel 16:13 "Then Samuel took the horn of oil, and anointed him in the midst of his brethren: and the Spirit of the LORD came upon David from that day forward." So Samuel rose up, and went to Ramah. Samuel anointed David with oil, when you have oil in your life no matter who tried to hold you down with persecution, oil and water doesn't mix and eventually the oil is coming to the top; Look at past persecutions as a set up and rise to the top and walk in your promotion. The promotion is a by-product of your kingdom performances 1 Samuel 17: 51 "Therefore David ran, and stood upon the Philistine, and took his sword, and drew it out of the sheath thereof, and slew him, and cut off his head in addition to that. And when the Philistines saw their champion was dead, they fled."

People desire to be seen, but they don't want to serve, submit or surrender. Some people want power but won't lay prostrate before God in prayer. The more prayer is released, the more power is received. Some are willing to seek out and settle for the accolades instead of suffering and enduring the agony of attacks that are the prerequisite for the pure anointing. David was a worshiper, warrior, working, and willing for God. Whenever the Lord gives an assignment, it is the completion of the assignment that sets you up for promotion. Your job performance and how well you conquer the assignment is what sets you up for the elevation. It's no time for playing when it's time for performance. God is looking for those that will pursue and perform the assignment to perfection. Whenever the Lord anoints you that anointing is task specific meaning that no one else can perform to perfection the assignment God has for your life. God has given you the authority to destroy and cut the head off of every one of your enemies. A sign of true victory is not for you to knock your enemy down, but it is the cut the head of your enemy off. David has made up in his mind that he is not letting anyone or anything hinder his performance. Make up your mind that no one or nothing is going to stop what God has assigned you to do. Saul tells David that he is no match for this champion, David responds by saying I have God on my side. "I can do all things through Christ that strengthens me," Philippians 4:13.

The person you will replace desires to put in you what has not worked for them just to see you fail. He tells him to put on his armor and David says your stuff hasn't been proven. David starts stripping off the armor that didn't fit. It's a dangerous thing to allow the person that you're getting ready to replace to put things on you, a sign that someone recognize they have been replaced is when they start putting on you for example lies, hating and criticism. David says your stuff isn't proven he says I have a testimony I've killed lions and bears, I already know what God is getting ready to do. With God on my side, I'm cutting the head of my enemy off. God is a God of strategy. God gave David a strategy and David defeated Goliath having five smooth stones and utilizing only one. Regardless of what you have to deal with you have the victory. After the battle comes promotion. Stay in the fight. You have the victory!

Printed in the United States
By Bookmasters